...for anyone moving on to
secondary school

"Everything seemed to be so much bigger than my last school. There were hundreds of boys, the school hall was enormous and I'm sure the teachers looked larger too! I was very fortunate because I had a friend who had been there for a year. Having a friend made all the difference!"
Brian Ogden, author

"On my first day at secondary school, I remember (with acute embarrassment) the first PE lesson. My mother, for reasons best known to herself, had put a seam up the middle of my gym skirt, thinking it was supposed to be a pair of shorts. I couldn't get them onto my legs and had to do the whole lesson (horror of horrors!) in my knickers!"
Moira Kean, BBC Producer

"There was a rumour that on the first day some new boys were put in the school dustbins. I spent the day in terror, fearing that I would end up in the bin. What a relief when the final bell went!"
Brian Sears, football statistician

Scripture Union, 207–209 Queensway, Bletchley, MK2 2EB, England.

© Scripture Union 2003 Reprinted 2003, 2004

ISBN 1 85999 757 0

British Library Cataloguing-in-Publication Data

A catalogue record for this book is available from the British Library.

Cover design by David Lund Design.
Internal design by David Lund Design.

Printed and bound in Malta by Interprint

Scripture quotations are from the Contemporary English Version © American Bible Society 1991, 1992, 1995. Used by permission/Anglicisations © British & Foreign Bible Society 1997.

With special thanks to Tim Cutting of the Bridgebuilder Trust, Nick Jeffery of Norfolk YMCA and Scripture Union schools workers.

This book
was given to

by

in preparation for secondary school

Date

My personal profile

Name

Date of birth

Height (without heels!)

Primary school

Favourite subject

Favourite teacher

Best friends

Secondary school

Form tutor

First day of term

Collect the signatures
of people you want to
remember!

A-Z
Survival Guide

Arguments

Moving schools can be a stressful time, so you are quite likely to lose your temper or get irritable. You may argue with your parents about your school uniform, or with old friends at school who are not spending so much time with you. If you're getting wound up, count to ten before you say anything, or walk away.

Assemblies

Like them or hate them, assemblies have to happen! In your new school they will probably be shorter and less fun. Some assemblies will include prayers or times of quiet. Use that opportunity to think about what was said and to think quietly or maybe pray for yourself and others.

Boys

There could be plenty of new boys to get to know and if you're a girl (and not going to a girls-only school!) that might be good or bad news! Some boys want to show off and many will seem immature. But others will be worth getting to know as friends. It's not worth trying to get a boyfriend too quickly – having lots of friends is much more fun!

Books

There are plenty of books and some will be great! The school library is a good place for homework or finding out information. Try to read what you need for each lesson and find good books that'll help with your studies and your life.

Idea: You might even want to see if the world's bestselling book has anything to say! (See page 63 to find out what it is.)

Bullying

Bullies are weak people. There's no excuse for bullying. If you think you're being bullied, don't let it go on. Tell a teacher, or someone else you can trust, immediately. That's the brave way to deal with cowards. Page 25 gives you some wise advice on this!

Break

A great time to let off steam, but takes some getting used to in a larger school. Try to stick with friends and stay in one place for a few days, until you feel confident to move around and mix a bit.

Brothers and sisters in school

If you have a brother or sister who is already at your new school, it can either be great, or pretty embarrassing! Teachers may read the list of names in the class and ask, "You're not related to HIM/HER, are you?" in a worried tone! They may expect you to be the super-human creep that he or she is. Don't worry – just be you, not anyone else.

Canteen

Moving to secondary school can mean you have a better choice of food at lunchtime. But when loads of young people get together to eat, it can be very noisy. If you use the dining room, watch what everyone else does. And try not to drop your tray on the first day!

Choices

You will have to make choices about many different things, including the friends you have, clubs you join, sports you play, or even the kind of lunch you eat! Later, you will have to choose subjects which could affect your future. Of course, there are also important choices to do with right and wrong. To make choices you need guidance, so talk to teachers, parents and friends. Many people ask God to help them make the right decisions.

Clubs

There will be plenty of clubs at your new school – chances to play more sport, make music or develop other interests. Make the most of these opportunities, but don't take on too much. You'll need time and energy for your home life and social life. Some schools have a Christian Union, which is a lunchtime or after-school club where young people go to find out more about God. You may think the CU is going to be boring or full of odd people. You may be wrong, but you'll never really know until you try!

Detention

Some schools keep students in at lunchtime or after school if they forget homework or break school rules. Detention is a waste of everyone's time, so it's best to keep out of it. If you do end up in detention, try to behave, or you'll end up in another one.

Drinks machine

There's a knack to using one! Watch someone else use it, and then copy exactly what they did. If the machine eats your money, make sure you know how to get it back (but no kicking!).

Drugs

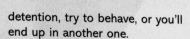

Illegal drugs are bad news. There may be a few students who want to persuade others to use drugs. They are always expensive and always harmful. It may be tempting to experiment, but drugs can cause illness and brain damage and cause users to lose control of themselves. If you come across them at school, walk away and report it – you'll be saving others from pain as well as yourself.

English

Language and literature courses cover how we speak and write the language. Some plays and novels may seem dull, but give them a chance. You might just find something you like. If you're really getting stuck with a book or a play you've got to study, why not see if there's a film made of it that you could watch?

Finding your way

Even if you do get lost, it's not the end of the world. Use the map of the school even if it is confusing! By the end of the first week, you'll know your way around. Always ask someone where you should go, rather than stumbling into a class of cool Year 10s! And try not to get separated from others in your class. Then you can all get lost together!

Form tutor

This is the teacher who checks the register and deals with any problems. Form tutors are usually chosen carefully because they are approachable and helpful. Don't be afraid to tell them if things are going wrong or if you feel bad about your first days at the school. They really are there to help.

Friends

If your friends are not going to the same school, you may feel a bit lost and lonely. But you won't be the only one. And friends from your old school may suddenly decide they've had enough of you as a friend! Very soon you'll probably find someone who has got things in common with you and a new friendship begins. If you make the effort to talk to others who seem to be on their own, you will find yourself making friends. Write a list of new friends after two weeks and see how well you have done.

Girls

Being in larger, mixed schools usually brings boys into contact with more girls. That can seem wonderful for boys! Often, however, most of the girls in the school will be older than you and most will not want to have anything to do with you. Try to get to know girls as friends and keep the friendships you had with the girls in your old school. Don't worry about getting your own 'girlfriend' yet. There's enough to get used to being in a new school without all that!

Heads

There are heads of subjects, heads of year, deputy heads, and the feared or famed head teacher (and don't forget the head lice!). All these teachers have special roles in school. They make sure you all learn and do well. Don't be scared of any of them! Tell them about anything that worries you.

Homework

There's no escape! Homework can be interesting, but it usually takes time. Get into the habit of doing it as soon as you get home and hand it in on time. Leave it too late and it can be hard to catch up. Use the homework timetable on page 62. Homework is a must – it may mean learning, completing exercises or writing notes. Your next lesson will usually follow on from the homework you've done.

Induction day

This is a really important day for you. Turn to page 61 for the induction day checklist!

Journey

Your school journey may be much longer and you're more likely to go by public transport. Allow enough time to get there in your first week. Being late will get you noticed for the wrong reasons. If you are late, give the honest reason why – teachers have heard all the false excuses before. On the school bus, you may think there's no-one to sit next to. But after a few days you're likely to have friends to sit with. The same is true if you walk to school. You'll meet up with others going the same way.

Kit

Remember when you need your PE or Games kit and make sure they are clean enough. There may be some kind of penalty at school if you don't have the correct kit at the correct time. So it is worth sorting out a routine right from the start. See PE and GAMES.

Loos

School toilets are not always the cleanest or most private places in the world! Make sure you discover where they are on your induction day and use them for what they were intended – and nothing else. They are not a good place to hide from lessons, as in most schools they are regularly visited by staff. ("So where is a good place?" we hear you cry. Well, we're not telling you!)

Loneliness

This is one of the biggest fears of moving on. But for most people it soon passes as you make new friends and mix in with others. Everyone feels lonely at different times. But if it really gets bad, talk to your form tutor about it. Many people also find a faith in God a real help when they're feeling lonely. Why not have a look at the Bible poem on page 46.

Maths   4 + 5 = 10

Maths is necessary for virtually all careers, so it is worth working at it and trying really hard. Don't forget that your teacher is there to help you, so ask if you don't understand.

4 + 5 = 10

Money

You'll find that you will always feel like you need more money than you actually have. But money is not always available, so decide what you really need and what you don't. You need money for lunch and bus fares, but don't take too much in case you lose it or it gets taken.

New

You will look and act 'new' for a few days. Starting somewhere new does give you a chance to put the past behind you and make a fresh start. If you start really well, you won't have to 'catch up' later on. Your new school is a great opportunity to make a positive new beginning. First impressions are important.

PE and Games

There will be more equipment and facilities and a variety of activities and games on offer. There will be more of a challenge. If you enjoy sport, you'll love it. If you don't, you might as well join in as there's really no choice anyway! Whatever the case, always try and do your best – we can't all be Olympic gold medallists. Getting changed for PE and Games can be embarrassing too. Remember that everyone develops physically at different speeds. Sport is not just for winners - exercise helps you to develop your physique and feel good about yourself. See KIT.

Office

The school office is a busy place, with the staff doing many jobs. Once you get used to the way the school office works, you will be confident about how to use it and how the staff can help you. Most office staff are very friendly!

Opportunities

WOW! What opportunities! More clubs, more subjects, more friends, trips to more places than would be possible in your old school! You may want to keep out of it all for a while, but once you are settled don't waste the opportunities school provides.

Parents

Despite being so old and out of touch, parents do want to know how their kids are getting on. They want you to succeed and be happy. If you're not, they will worry. Try to let them help you by talking to them about the good things and the hard things too. If you are finding it really hard, ask them to speak to school for you. See page 23.

PSE and Citizenship

Personal and social education (PSE) covers a range of subjects looking at how you develop as a person. It includes health, relationships and sex, developing confidence and making the most of your abilities. Through PSE you should learn that it is OK to be different and have beliefs which others don't share. Citizenship helps you become an informed and active citizen in our society, looking at things such as the law and police, social issues and politics.

Rules

All schools have rules and sanctions. Most are for the safety and well-being of all the students. You may even get a chance to create your own form rules. Rules are there to follow rather than to break. Find out what they are and stick to them from the start. If you don't, you may find yourself with things like detentions, report cards and letters home to your parents... not a good start!

Religious Education (RE)

Faith, religion and spirituality are as vital to people as the question of their roots or history. It is important to understand different faiths, and how they influence attitudes and behaviour. You will explore different religions, beliefs, values, and ceremonies, and learn to respect others. Christians believe in God and follow his ways, as shown in the Bible. They believe that Jesus came to show us what God is like and to show us how God wants us to live our lives.

Quiet people

It's great that we're all different! Some people seem quiet; others really loud. Many quiet people are thinkers who don't say much but listen to louder people making fools of themselves! There is nothing wrong with being quiet. Sometimes people are loud because they're nervous or insecure. And if you are more of an extrovert, just be yourself. But don't forget to be sensitive to others. Quiet people also make good friends because they listen to your problems.

Swimming

Some schools provide swimming lessons, while others have swimming clubs. Swimming is a great way to get fit and provides opportunities for races and team membership. You may find changing for swimming a bit embarrassing, but once you're in the water what you or your costume or trunks are like doesn't matter.

Size

Look around the hall, full of all the new pupils. You'll see some boys and girls who look almost fully grown, and others who look like small children. Everyone develops at a different rate. If you are smaller or less physically developed, don't worry. You'll have your growth spurt.

Timetable

Your new school timetable tells you what subject you do, where and at what time. It may seem complicated, but as long as you copy it down correctly it will soon make sense.

Trainers

Trainers may not be on your school's regulation uniform list! But they are a fashion statement and wearing the wrong make or the wrong design can sometimes lead to people taking the mickey. Try not to be too caught up by the fashion thing, and be your own person instead. See BULLIES.

Teachers

You are likely to have many more teachers, with a different one for every subject. Some teachers seem less friendly than others, but don't let that put you off their subject. Teachers are there to help you learn, so ask them questions or tell them if you don't understand things. Try to remember that teachers are normal people, with problems and moods just like you! If you want a laugh, read *My Teacher* on page 21.

Tests and exams

Tests and exams are part of school life. As you get older they will help you decide what you are good at and what you may want to do in the future. All you can do is your best. You will do better if you've prepared for them and you don't panic.

Uniform

Your new school uniform may be more formal and strict than you are used to. Schools usually have uniforms to make the students feel united and look moderately smart. The rules will be clear on what you can and can't wear.

Web site

Many larger schools now have their own web sites and many of the questions you would like to ask will be on it. There may also be more up-to-date information than in the prospectus, with news about school trips, sports competitions and staff changes. Web sites are a great way to access information, so it is well worth a look.

Youngest

Being the youngest in school (and possibly the smallest) could make you feel vulnerable and scared. By this time next year, however, you'll feel settled and confident, while next year's newest pupils will be feeling as you do now. Being the youngest does give you more excuses for being late or getting lost on the way to lessons!

Zits

The time you change school coincides with adolescence, when you and your body are changing. Zits and spots are unavoidable as you grow up, but if you keep your face clean by washing it regularly, and eat fruit and vegetables, you can stop them getting too bad. A few people may get them really badly (this is usually called acne) but your doctor should be able to offer some help if this is the case.

Top Ten Answers!

781 children in the United Kingdom, who are about to move on to secondary schools, were asked these three questions. Their answers made up the top ten charts on the next few pages.

- What is the best thing about your new school?
- What will you miss most of all about your old school?
- What is the most scary thing about your new school?

How would you answer these questions? Turn over to see if your answers are in the Top Ten! Here are comments from three children in Bolton.

"On the visit, I liked my form tutor and getting things to do in geography. But I disliked some older children because they pushed me in the ice-cream queue! I want to be in the school football team. My dream is to be a footballer." Justin Hill

"I'm looking forward to my new school because it's bigger and it's got more rooms and I'll get a different teacher for every lesson. I wouldn't like it if I didn't make any friends. I'm looking forward to playing either a cornet or a trumpet, and after-school clubs. When I get older, I would like to be a lawyer and drive a silver Jaguar." Chloe Sherwood

"I like my new secondary school because it's got interesting sports. I can't find anything I dislike except for the fact that it's falling apart! On my visit I did rock-climbing and abseiling. That was fun. I also met some teachers. They were kind. I want to become either a policeman, a lawyer or a pilot." Kamran Afhal

Thanks to the children from Balvanich Primary (Isle of Benbecula); Cairnshill Primary (S Belfast); Coppull St John's Primary (Lancashire); Gibson Primary (Omagh); Gilnow Primary (Bolton); Hillview Primary (Hucclecote, Gloucester); Kingsland School (Bangor, N Ireland); Loughton Middle School (Milton Keynes); Mellor Primary (Leicester); many Nottinghamshire Primary Schools who know Nick Harding!; St Anthony's RC Primary (Watford); St John's C of E Primary (Sparkhill, Birmingham); St John's C of E Primary (Brinscall, Lancashire); St John's C of E Primary (Whittle-le-Woods, Lancashire); St Joseph's RC Primary School (Carryduff, N Ireland); St Mary's C of E Primary (Kirtbury, W Berks); Swanbourne House School (Milton Keynes).

What is the best thing about your new school?

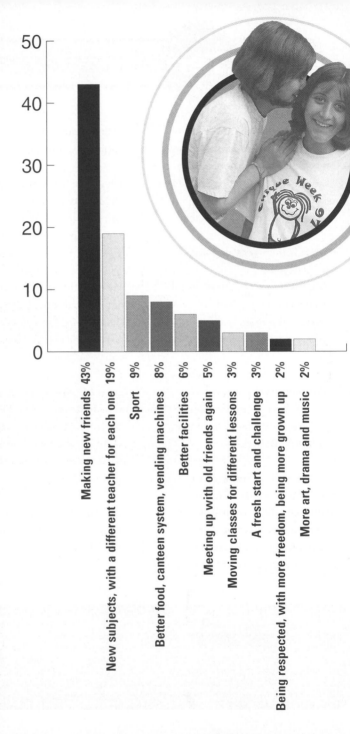

Making new friends 43%

New subjects, with a different teacher for each one 19%

Sport 9%

Better food, canteen system, vending machines 8%

Better facilities 6%

Meeting up with old friends again 5%

Moving classes for different lessons 3%

A fresh start and challenge 3%

Being respected, with more freedom, being more grown up 2%

More art, drama and music 2%

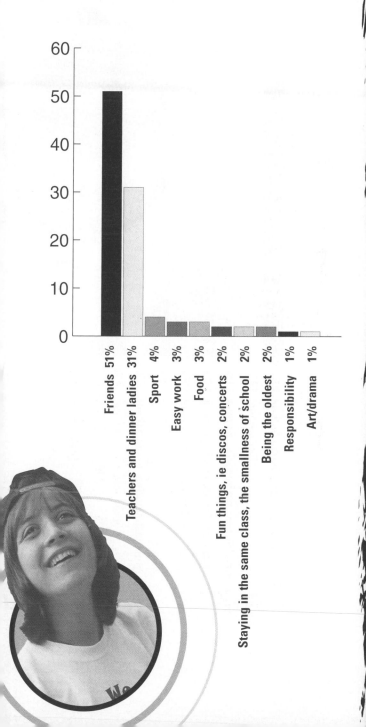

Friends	51%
Teachers and dinner ladies	31%
Sport	4%
Easy work	3%
Food	3%
Fun things, ie discos, concerts	2%
Staying in the same class, the smallness of school	2%
Being the oldest	2%
Responsibility	1%
Art/drama	1%

What will you miss most of all about your old school?

What is the most scary thing about your new school?

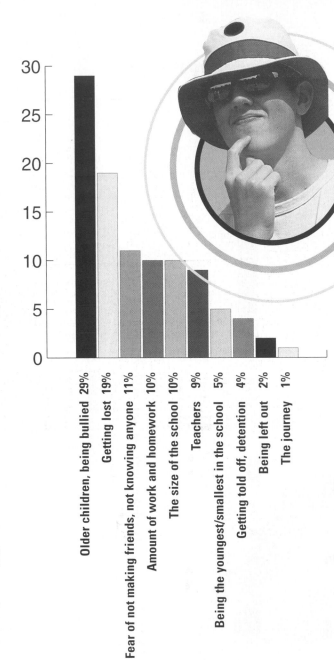

- Older children, being bullied 29%
- Getting lost 19%
- Fear of not making friends, not knowing anyone 11%
- Amount of work and homework 10%
- The size of the school 10%
- Teachers 9%
- Being the youngest/smallest in the school 5%
- Getting told off, detention 4%
- Being left out 2%
- The journey 1%

My teacher

My teacher once wore nappies
My teacher used to crawl
My teacher used to cry at night
My teacher used to bawl.

My teacher jibber
jabbered
My teacher ran up
stairs
My teacher wrote
in squiggles
My teacher stood
on chairs.

My teacher once was
naughty
My teacher was so rude
My teacher used a bad
word
My teacher spilled her food.

My teacher lost her homework
My teacher took too long
My teacher got detention
My teacher did things wrong.

My teacher's all grown-up now
My teacher can't recall
My teacher thinks she's different
My teacher's not at all.

Taken from *The Day I Fell Down the Toilet*, by Steve
Turner, Lion Publishing. Reproduced with permission.

Friends

Friends are like fire,
spreading across vast
areas
and reaching out for
everything in its path.
But when something
new and different
comes along – like
water,
it can all extinguish
with one blast
so your friendship is
left as history, as ash.
But sometimes there's
a spark.
If you save that spark,
you can light it again.
Your friendship can
start again,
slowly return to what
you had.

Daisy Shirley-Beavan (10),
from *Our poems and no
messin'*, © Scripture Union
1999.

You're still you

You're swapping your recorder for a rock guitar
You've put a centre parting in your hair.
You've thrown away those CDs with the nice songs on,
And black's the only colour that you'll wear.

You look at me as though I'm sad, or even worse,
As though I'm getting past my sell-by date.
You need me as your taxi-driver every night,
But you don't want me at that new school gate.

But you're still you and I'm still me,
Just two people getting by.
Making our way in this world so wide,
Can we still walk side by side?

OK, so I'm your mother and right down deep
Are some complicated feelings for you.
I want you to be happy and I know I can't keep
You a child for ever. What should I do?

So let me go slowly, tell me I'm cool,
That we're just two people finding a way
To pass through changes in this world so
wide
And still walk side by side.

Can we still walk side by side?

© Gill Saxon, 2000

Gill wrote this when her daughter,
Emma, was about to move to
Impington Village College in
Cambridge.

Come to the edge.

We might fall.

Come to the edge.

It's too high!

Come to the edge

And they came

and he pushed

and they flew.

This poem was quoted by Mary McAleese in her inaugural address as the President of the Irish Republic, when she was urging people to take risks and to trust.

'Come to the Edge' by Christopher Logue from *Selected Poems*, Faber and Faber. Reproduced with permission.

What shall I do?
Help!

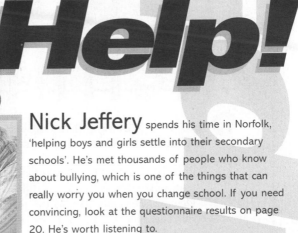

Nick Jeffery spends his time in Norfolk, 'helping boys and girls settle into their secondary schools'. He's met thousands of people who know about bullying, which is one of the things that can really worry you when you change school. If you need convincing, look at the questionnaire results on page 20. He's worth listening to.

It's funny, isn't it, that staff at secondary school sometimes give you the wrong message. Take bullying, for instance! There you are, in the main hall during your first week listening to a dull (sorry), exciting lecture (oops), I mean friendly chat from the Head of Year. They're talking about how this school has not had an instance of bullying since 1875, but if you are bullied, see someone who can really help you! They may even say, "There are no bullies in this school!" Now that is risky, because if you are bullied, you will think it must be your fault. The truth is, every school has bullies. If you think about it, I bet you've been bullied before. And if you're really honest, you've probably bullied someone yourself too! (Yes, even someone as angelic as you!) Believe it or not, being bullied is not the real problem; it's what you do about it that counts.

There is an unwritten rule in school amongst pupils that says, "Never tell on a bully!" Why not? Who says? Doesn't it just make things worse, mess up the victim's life and make the bully think he or she can get away with it? Or have I missed the point? Being bullied can make us feel really lonely. Some pupils won't tell anyone at all. They just stay silent and suffer. There is an episode of The Simpsons — you know, the one where Nelson is bullying Bart. He is being 'got' after school. He sits in the classroom all day, terrified but not doing anything about it. At the end of school he tries to run away but Nelson is waiting and beats him up. Nelson tells him that he will get beaten up every day after school! Eventually Bart does something about it.

What would you do? Have a look at 'Dilemmas' and see how you get on...

Dilemmas

1 Your mate is being pushed around by some big kids and calls to you for help. What do you do?

- [ ] A Pretend you didn't hear anything and scurry off to your next class.
- [ ] B Dive in, like Superman, to the rescue only to limp out five minutes later with more than your pride hurt.
- [ ] C Ask an adult in school to sort it out.

2 Someone in your tutor group has started picking on you and has threatened to beat you up after school. What will you do?

- [ ] A Spend all day worrying about it instead of concentrating on your lessons, and pray that they will forget.
- [ ] B Face the bully and threaten them with worse stuff.
- [ ] C Wait for the end of tutor time, then quietly explain what is going on to your tutor or an adult you trust.

3 Your friend rushes into the tutor group, late. There's a long piece of loo paper hanging out of the back of his trousers. Do you...

- [ ] A Fall about in hysterics, with everybody else?
- [ ] B Drag him outside before anyone sees?
- [ ] C Report it so that the teacher can deal with this serious matter?

4 In Science, you overhear two of your tutor group whispering about a secret you shared with just your best friend. What will you do?

☐ A Say nothing and stop being best friends.
☐ B Make up some things about your friend and tell everyone to get your own back.
☐ C Confront your friend, hear their side of the story, then decide what to do.

5 You find some kids in the toilets, blocking the sinks and turning on the taps. They see you and tell you to ignore it, "or else!". Do you...

☐ A Ignore it?
☐ B Stop the flood by unblocking the sinks yourself?
☐ C Find an adult immediately?

How did you get on?

Mostly A – OK, so you like to play it safe, but watch out. You may become a doormat or you could be in danger of being bullied yourself. You have rights and are special. Try to be more like C.

Mostly B – Woah! You throw caution to the wind and get stuck in there. Slow down, take a deep breath and think before you act or you could find yourself in big trouble at school.

Mostly C – You're not scared to speak out about what's going on around you. Once a bully sees you can't be intimidated, they'll soon give up. But you don't have to report everything to a teacher. Some things you can deal with yourself - like stray loo paper!

So, was it as bad as you expected?

So, was it as bad as you
So, was
So, was it as bad as you expected?

Sophie Friend had mixed feelings about going up to secondary school. "I was scared that I might not make any friends and that I'd get bullied, though I was excited too because it was such a big step in my life."

So, how did Sophie survive? Did she make friends? You bet she did. Her social diary is currently booked solid and she's having the best time ever!

Geoff Miller thought he'd keep getting lost when he started senior school. It was humungous; ten times bigger than his primary school: "It was like a maze. Endless corridors, hundreds of rooms, thousands of people."

"But it was fine because in Year 7 all my lessons were in the same rooms. I never got lost once. And now I know my way around the whole school."

Danielle Wade was worried about her speling, sorry, spelling! She thought the teechers would get mad at her for making misteaks.

Did they? "No, they were really nice. They kept giving me commendations to encourage me. I got bundles of them. In Year 7 you've only got to blow your nose and someone will give you a commendation for it. But make the most of it. They don't bother once you get into Year 8!"

Jonathan Hulin was a bit scared he'd have the mickey taken out of him because he hated sports – all sports – but especially football. Also, because he was tall and skinny, he dreaded the communal showers. He suffered agonies just thinking about it.

"It was hard at first. Some people used to call me names like 'Twiglet' and stuff, but my real friends stuck by me. I played football because I had to but, by the end of the autumn term, I realised I didn't hate it any more. I actually looked forward to it. And now that I play regularly, I'm not so skinny any more. I've got muscles!"

Mega wordsearch

Can you find all these words in the grid?

Secondary
Timetable
School
IT
CD ROM
Bus
Classroom
Teacher
Canteen
Trainers
Homework
Friends
Exam
Uniform
Pen
Ruler
Tutor
Book
Library
Art
Maths
PE
Chips
Form
SATS

T	I	M	E	T	A	B	L	E	T
E	C	D	R	O	M	K	J	U	R
A	X	R	U	L	E	R	T	I	A
C	L	A	S	S	R	O	O	M	I
H	A	B	M	A	R	W	P	R	N
E	L	N	U	T	E	E	B	O	E
R	I	O	T	S	P	M	O	F	R
O	B	F	O	E	C	O	O	I	S
M	R	O	F	H	E	H	K	N	N
M	A	T	H	S	C	N	I	U	E
F	R	I	E	N	D	S	L	P	P
A	Y	R	A	D	N	O	C	E	S

29

It's your mooooove groooove

Now this is a story about an ordinary guy
Whose small school life had passed him by.
He had had a great time – life full of tricks,
But now it-was-the-end! Bye-bye Year 6!

When the time came, he'd not know how he'd feel
To be a very small cog in a very big wheel.
He'd… not… know – what… it was to be,
Just a very small fish in a very big sea.

Mooooooviiiing – it's a bit scary,
It's a bit new.
Mooooooviing – just remember,
To be YOU!

September was here and it started bad.
The place was big – timetable mad.
He found he'd be lost when the bell would ring
And the stairs seemed to move like the Harry Potter thing.

But after a while, he got to know
To join in, chill out – and go with the flow.
He'd no longer worry about the pain in the neck
When Year 12s came by, even bigger than Shrek.

Mooooooviiiing – it's a bit scary,
It's a bit new.
Mooooooviing – just remember,
To be YOU!

Half term soon came and he'd have to say
He could still remember that scary first day,
But he had his new friends and new things to do
And even the teachers were quite human too.

Mooooooviiiing – it's a bit scary,
It's a bit new.
Mooooooviing – just remember,
To be YOU!

Just remember – TO BE YOU

Bob Miles

Dolphins

Jessica stood in the wings, shaking with nerves, waiting for her cue. June the first. Day of the dress rehearsal. She'd been dreading it for weeks. Might as well be April the first. She desperately didn't want to make a fool of herself. She took some deep, slow breaths, and went over her words: 'Romeo, Romeo! Wherefore art thou Romeo? Deny thy father and refuse thy name...'

Hidden behind a curtain, she could overhear Sasha and Angie gossiping. She knew they were just jealous, but that didn't make it any easier.

'You should've seen Greg Robertson's face when he heard he was going to be Romeo, and she was going to be Juliet!' Sasha whispered. Jessica could hear them sniggering.

'She only got the part because Miss Brown recommended her to Mr Nevis,' Angie hissed.

'What, Miss Brown the dance teacher?'

'Yep. Jessica used to be in the dance troop, you know. Miss Brown said she was a good mover.'

'Like Dumbo, you mean?' Sasha snorted.

Jessica knew why she'd been picked. She had a good, loud voice, and she wasn't scared. At least, that's what everyone thought. She'd spent years building up her street cred, making everyone believe she wasn't frightened of anything at all. It was true that she wasn't scared of any of the kids in the playground. She could make mincemeat of most of them, and she'd proved it once or twice, until she'd begun to understand more about anger, and how Jesus could help her with it. But a whole audience was a different matter. They could make mincemeat of her. And they probably would.

It was true, she used to dance. She'd grown too heavy for ballet in primary school, but she'd transferred to disco and jazz and been a star for a while. Miss Brown reckoned it was her natural Caribbean sense of rhythm. Then she became too aware of her body and felt too shy to dance any more. Right now, she felt miserable and very lonely. 'Ready, Jess?' Mr Nevis asked. 'Don't worry. It's only the dress rehearsal.'

Exactly, Jessica thought. If it had been the real thing, for mums and dads, it would have been OK. They always liked things. But out there was the whole of her year. Nearly two hundred kids. They would probably eat her alive.

'Remember, Jess. Up on to the balcony. One step forward. Pause, and speak! Up you go now!'

Jessica climbed cautiously up the stepladder that led to the scene's balcony, holding her long dress out of the way of her feet. She always felt awkward in anything but joggers and a T-shirt, and here she was wearing some flimsy, floaty thing, slung over one shoulder and held on with tacking stitches and pins.

She reached the top step, and ventured out along the plank. Step. Pause. Speak! 'Romeo! Romeo! Wherefore art thou Romeo?' Her voice wobbled. Someone in the audience giggled. The hem of the dress was caught. Jessica shuffled, trying to free it. There was an ear-piercing crack, and she made a grab for the curtain just as the entire balcony collapsed. She fell, tangled up in the dress and the curtain.

There was a horrified silence, and everyone held their breath. Then Jessica fought her way from under curtains and pieces of wood with one knee scraped and her pride in tatters. Her floaty dress had been torn off in the fall, and she found herself alone in the middle of the stage in her bra and pants.

There was another split second's silence, then the whole room erupted in shrieks of delight. Jessica fled to the costume room, pulled on her joggers and T-shirt, grabbed her school bag in one hand and her trainers in the other, and ran for her life, unaware of Mr Nevis's concerned voice behind her. 'Jess! Any damage done? Jessica!'

Jessica sprinted out of the building, pausing at the school gates only long enough to stuff her feet into her trainers, Then she ran home and arrived shocked and breathless.

'Hello, honey!' said her mum, looking up from a casserole of something hot and spicy. 'Been running? You're early! How did the dress rehearsal go?'

'Er, the scenery wasn't ready, so we didn't do it all.'

'I'm so looking forward to tomorrow,' Mum said happily. She loved performances. She dressed up for every occasion, and made an entrance like the Queen of Sheba, just as if it was she who was on the stage. Just thinking about it made Jessica cringe. 'I know I've seen you in lots of dance shows,' Mum went on, 'but this will be your first play!' The phone rang, and Mum went into the hall to answer it. Jessica fled to her bedroom. How was she ever going to tell Mum that she wouldn't be acting tomorrow evening, or ever again. In fact, she was never, ever going to set foot in that school again in her whole life.

'Jessica?' Mum was lumbering up the stairs. 'That was the school. They said you'd fallen. They wanted to know if you're OK.'

Jessica wanted to cry, but since she never cried she kicked the foot of her bed so hard it made the wall shake. Mum demanded to know what was wrong. Since Jessica's mum was heavier than Jessica and as immovable as a brick wall, Jessica had no choice but to describe the whole afternoon to her, all except for the dress. 'I think the scenery collapsed because I'm too fat and heavy for it. It was designed for Juliet, not for an elephant!' she growled.

'Now let's get one thing straight!' said Mum firmly. 'You're not fat! You're strong and fit and healthy. All the swimmin' and joggin' you do has made muscle, not fat. And you're a very graceful mover. Miss Brown always said so. And just because you're not the right build for ballet any more doesn't mean you aren't very gifted!'

'Maybe I'll become a gifted demolition expert,' Jessica sniffed. 'Silly!' Mum said, giving her a hug. 'Something'll turn up. Every cloud has a silver linin'. Now come down and have somethin' to eat.'

'I'll be down in a minute, Mum. I'll just get changed.' But when Mum had gone, the full horror of the gossip and the laughter hit Jessica again. Mum didn't have to listen to Sasha and Angie being rude, or face Greg Robertson, or cope with the whole year talking about her knickers. And they surely would. Endlessly. She sat miserably on her bed and looked around. She'd forgotten to turn the page of her calendar. It was still on May. She looked at the picture. It was a mother hen gathering her chicks safely under her wing while outside the wire of the hen-house was a fox who couldn't get at them. There was a Bible verse underneath: 'Hide me in the shadow of your wings.' The calendar was from Aunty Ali. She always sent calendars and cards with Bible verses on them.

Jessica flipped the page to June, and the picture was a cartoon. There was a guy who was obviously full of himself, standing tall and arrogant, and a little, shy, dumpy figure, afraid to look up. But the sun was shining brightly on the second figure, and the Bible verse read, 'People judge others by what they look like, but the Lord judges people by what is in their hearts.' That's all very well, Lord, Jessica thought. But what's the good of wantin' to do things well, and havin' a beautiful heart, if you just look like a puddin'?

Having changed and washed her face Jessica went downstairs, but the smell of spicy chicken and pineapple didn't do anything for her. 'I don't think I need any food just now, Mum.'

'What's the matter, love? You sickenin' for something?'

Sickening. Yes, that was the word. Jessica rushed out and threw up in the bathroom.

The next day was Thursday, and Jessica didn't actually feel sick at all, but she figured that if she remained ill she didn't have to go to school, and her understudy could play Juliet. It gave her time to think out some sort of strategy. So she said she felt queasy and refused breakfast and lunch. Her sister, Marina, looked disbelieving, but didn't grass on her.

Jessica stuffed yesterday's pants and bra into her waste bin, hoping never to set eyes on them again, but beyond that she had no idea what to do. She could run away, but that wouldn't be fair on Mum, and anyway, where would she go?

Maybe she could change schools? But the next nearest one was two bus rides away, in a rough area. Back to square one in building up the street cred. Jessica shuddered.

On Friday and Saturday she stayed in her room, though she did go down to the kitchen for meals. 'Why don't you go out for a gentle jog?'

Mum suggested. 'A bit of fresh air might do you good.'

Jessica scowled. 'I might meet someone who... who...''

On Sunday afternoon, Mum said brightly, 'Remember Sylvia from work?' Jessica nodded. 'She's a member of the Country Club Leisure Complex. She can get guests in for just a couple of pounds to use the pool. Do you want to go?'

Jessica wavered. She'd love a swim, and she'd be unlikely to meet anyone she knew at the Country Club. It was mostly posh people who went there. 'There's a sauna, and a jacuzzi,' Mum added. Mum was planning to swim, and the sight of Jessica's mother in a swimsuit was enough to draw attention away from Jessica.

'OK. I'll get my things.' She wondered if Mum would tell Sylvia about 'Romeo and Juliet.'

The Country Club pool was beautiful. There were flumes and a kids' pool, a diving area, and plenty of room for real swimming. Palm trees and tables around the edge reminded Jessica of photos of Jamaica. Home, Mum always called it.

Mum and Sylvia chatted at the shallow end while Jessica dived into the deep end and raced up and down the length, revelling in fast action after so many days of inactivity. The pool was almost empty. Jessica dived again and again, swimming almost a length underwater before coming up for air, then turning and varying her strokes – crawl, butterfly, breaststroke, life-saving backstroke. She imagined pearl divers aiming as deep as they could, over and over, in the hope of a perfect pearl. She'd heard that some could last four minutes without a breath. She thought of turquoise sea, soft white sand and pink coral. She dived and glided, then twisted and somersaulted in a personal underwater acrobatic display.

When she came up for air, Mum and Sylvia were heading for the sauna. A girl about Jessica's age seemed to be watching her from the edge of the pool. Jessica shook the water out of her eyes and peered. With relief, she felt certain she didn't know her, so she dived again, enjoying being alone.

Next time she paused there was a young woman with the girl, and they were definitely looking at her. In panic, Jessica wondered if she was doing something wrong. She was wearing a wrist-band, she'd showered before swimming, there wasn't a NO DIVING sign. What could it be? But the young woman smiled, and the girl slid gracefully into the water and swam up to Jessica.

'Hi!' she said, 'I'm Anna. Sorry to stare at you like that. It's just that you, well, the way you were diving... I mean, you're brilliant!' She laughed. 'No, really! Where did you learn to swim like that?'

'I, er, well, I learnt to swim when I was little,' Jessica stuttered, 'but I don't know...' They arrived at the side of the pool. The young woman who was with Anna squatted down. 'Hello, I'm Carrie. I coach the synchronised swimming team, and Anna came to fetch me because she said you're a natural! And from what I've just seen, she's right.' Jessica stared. She didn't know what to say.

'Synchronised swimming. It's like ballet in the water, swimming in formation,' Carrie explained.

'Er, yes. I've seen it on TV. They do it in the Olympics, don't they?' Jessica climbed out to sit on the edge. 'Er, I'm Jessica. I haven't been before. My mum's friend's a member...'

'Have you ever done any synchro?' Anna asked.

'No, but I've done some racin'. Never came first, though.'
'Synchronised swimming isn't about speed,' Carrie explained. 'It's about control and grace. And you've got both. And with some training with the team, who knows where you could go! Will you come and try?

We practise here on Tuesday evenings at 7 o'clock.'

'Tuesday evenin', that's when, er, yes! I'd love to!' What a perfect excuse not to go to the drama club! 'Er, thanks!' she said to Carrie.

'Don't thank me. Thank Anna. She's the talent spotter.'

Jessica grinned at Anna.

'We're called the Dolphins,' Anna added.

'Dolphins?'

'Yep! Because they're the most graceful creatures in the water – very intelligent, and they look after each other – work as a team.'

Jessica thought of the shape of dolphins. Then she considered Anna's description. Graceful, intelligent and good team members.

'You'll like it!' Anna assured her.

'Thanks,' Jessica replied. 'I think I might!'

'What's up with you?' Daleep asked Arun as they washed up the dinner dishes. 'You haven't said a word all week. That must be a record, even for you!'

'Nothing,' Arun lied. In fact, he was worried about Jessica. She'd been off school for two days after her fall at the dress rehearsal. When she'd returned to school the following Monday, he'd expected her to have her arm in a sling, or to be walking with crutches, but she seemed fine. She wasn't even limping.

Since his conversation with her on the day of the flour bag incident, he'd realised she wasn't all fists and a thick skull. He hated all the gossip and fun-poking. He wanted to tell everyone to shut up, but he didn't have the guts.

'Must be girl problems,' Daleep jibed.

'No!' Arun said, rather too quickly.

'Ah-ha!' Daleep ginned. 'So it is girl problems. Let me guess. Sasha?

She's in your class, isn't she? Or Angie...'

'Gimme a break!' Arun growled.

'So, who else could it be? Ella? No, she's with Phil.'

'How do you know?' Arun asked, amazed.

'Oh, I keep my ear to the ground,' Daleep replied mysteriously. 'How about the musical one? What's her name? Claire? No, you wouldn't stand a chance. How about that big girl, Jessica? The one who can slay three boys at a time with one hand behind her back!'

Arun didn't say anything, but his expression must have given him away because Daleep pounced. 'It is her! You wanna be careful, mate. That one barks and bites!'

'She doesn't!' Arun objected.

Daleep looked amused. Arun was mad. 'She's, she's...' He wanted to stick up for Jessica without giving away anything of the conversation he'd found so helpful. 'Actually, she's very thoughtful. I share a desk with her in FCT. And she's a good actress. She's got a great voice.'

Daleep still looked amused, but there was no mockery in his eyes now. 'Go on,' he urged, laying down his dish towel.

'Well, it's just that, um...'

'You don't know what to say to her?'

'No! Yes. Well, sort of...' Arun looked at Daleep. He expected a list of clever chat-up lines, but the usual hardness had gone from Daleep's expression. Encouraged, he went on, 'She fell. In a drama rehearsal. It was a bad fall. She's quite, um, heavy. And she had a couple of days off school. Everyone laughed about it. Since she came back, she doesn't seem to talk to anyone, and she's left the drama club.'

'And you want to know if she's OK?'

'Yeah!'

'Well, mate, I can assure you, she's fine!' Daleep grinned and punched Arun gently on the shoulder.

'How do you know?'

'She's in the synchronised swimming team at the Country Club Leisure Complex.'

'Where you're on placement?'

'Yep!'

'Are you sure it's her?'

'She's a bit hard to miss, right?'

Arun grinned and nodded.

'What's more, she's good,' Daleep added. 'Tell you what. Why don't you come with me on Tuesday and watch them? It's mostly just mums that stay and watch, but you could sit in the café and have a coke or something.'

On Tuesday evening, Daleep got permission to take Arun along to the Leisure Centre. While Daleep went off to supervise the Pulse Centre, Arun bought a fizzy drink and a chocolate bar at the Country Club café and sat at one of the tables beside the pool. There was a group of mums chatting and drinking coffee at the table next to him, and he took refuge behind them. He didn't want to be too obvious.

The girls trooped out of the changing rooms and jumped into the pool, ducking and diving, and generally warming up. They were wearing the same swimsuits, black with a sort of wavy white stripe up the side and white swimming hats. Jessica looked great.

As Arun watched, the coach stepped forward and put the girls through their paces, swimming lengths, using different strokes. Jessica glided through the water with no splash at all.

Then the girls formed a circle, skulling on their backs like the spokes of a wheel, their toes almost touching in the middle. At a signal, they each lifted one leg, perfectly straight, pointing their feet at the ceiling, still in circular formation. Then they did backward somersaults, absolutely coordinated, surfacing holding hands, arms outstretched.

Arun forgot about hiding. He craned his neck to get a better view. The display was amazing. He didn't know how these girls could do it, all together, with hardly a ripple in the water. Jessica was stunning. In the water, she didn't look at all large and ungainly. In fact, she had a good, curvy figure. The water shone and glistened on her skin. And she was such a fantastic swimmer – elegant and graceful. She made everything look easy.

Wanting to encourage her, as she had encouraged him, Arun thought about what to say. He'd tell her she was ace. A great swimmer. A winner. So, at the end of the session, when some of the mums stepped forward to hand towels to their daughters and say well done, Arun stepped forward, too.

Jessica obviously hadn't spotted him earlier. 'Hey, Arun! What're you doin' here?'

'Just came to watch,' he grinned. 'Jess, you were, um, I just thought, er, you're beautiful!' He gasped. That wasn't what he'd planned to say.

Jessica looked stunned for a moment, then she smiled broadly, tugged off her white swimming hat, and shook drops of water from her crinkly hair all over Arun. Laughing, she pranced off to the changing room, but just before she went in, she turned back to look at him. She was still smiling, and she mouthed 'thanks' before she disappeared inside.

Books from Scripture Union

Fabulous Phoebe
by Kathy Lee
1 85999 678 7
£3.99

Phoebe has got LOTS of questions: what is the creepy bird-woman up to? How can she show her face at school after the Awful Babysitting Incident? And most importantly, how on earth can she get Leo Jones to like her?
Look out for the other three books in the series.

The Last Straw & More
by Helen Parker
1 85999 646 9
£3.99

Ten great stories to really get your teeth into!
Food and Consumer Technology was never Arun's best subject… and then he had a run-in with a wobbly stepladder and a bag of flour. Phil wants to be Ella's date for the Valetine's Disco, but he's got competition. And will Gemma stick by her friend when a crisis in Holly's family means there's disaster around every corner?

Blood on the Wall
by Tony Dobinson
1 85999 639 6 £3.99

A blind beggar has been brutally stabbed to death. Nobody seems to care, but Jeb is determined to discover the killer. As he gets closer to the truth, danger lurks down every alley. Can Jeb solve the puzzle before the knife catches up with him? Your challenge – should you decide to accept it – is to find the murderer before it's too late!

Following *He Should Have Looked Behind Him*, this is the second adventure of Jeb Bar Benjamin.

All these books are available from your local Christian bookshop, from Scripture Union Mail Order, 01908 856006, or online at www.scriptureunion.org.uk

OK

- we know that you love doodling on your schoolbooks so here's a place where you can doodle to your heart's content without getting told off. Why not get your best friends to draw a cartoon of themselves to remind you of them when you move on to your next school?

doo

my mate Jo

lling

You have looked deep into my heart, Lord,
and you know all about me.
You know when I am resting and when I am
working,
and from heaven you discover my thoughts.

You notice everything I do and everywhere I go.
Before I even speak a word
you know what I will say
and with your powerful arm
you protect me from every side.
I can't understand all this!
Such knowledge is far above me.

Where could I go to escape
from your Spirit or from your sight?
If I were to climb up to the highest heavens,
you would be there.
If I were to dig down to the world of the dead
you would also be there.

Suppose I had wings like the dawning
day
and flew across the ocean.
Even then your powerful arm
would guide and protect me.
Or suppose I said, "I'll hide in the dark
until night comes to cover me over."
But you see in the dark
because daylight and dark are all the
same to you.

You are the one who put me together
inside my mother's body,
and I praise you
because of the wonderful way you created
me.
Everything you do is marvellous!
Of this I have no doubt.

Nothing about me is hidden from you!
I was secretly woven together
deep in the earth below,
but with your own eyes
you saw my body being formed.
Even before I was born, you had written in your book
        everything I would do.

This poem is actually taken from a book called the Bible and can be found in a section called Psalms (psalm means 'song'). Life is like a book, made up of many chapters. In your life, the previous one is about to end and the next one is about to begin. And it is a very important one. You are in for big, big changes. All the future lies ahead. But, at the same time, you can't help thinking about the past.

King David, who probably wrote this poem, knew all about making big mistakes in the past and he knew all about getting worried about the future too. But what stopped him from getting overwhelmed and creeping into a corner to hide was that he knew God was with him everywhere he went and whoever he was with. That's not a scary thought because there was no need to try to hide from God. After all, God knew all about him, even from before he was born. He knew how David would turn out and would protect him. David's life was so full of adventures that he certainly needed that protection!

David was a king who lived nearly three thousand years ago. But what he said about God then is still true! People who read David's songs and poems in the Bible have always loved Psalm 139. They know God notices everything about them and wants the very best for them. It's true for you too, as you begin the next chapter of your life.

When it all gets too much!

If, after reading everything in this book, you're still feeling a bit stressed, here's a page which will give you a bit of light relief!

There were two snakes. One said to the other, "Hey, are we poisonous?"
"No," he said.
"That's a relief," said the first, "I've just bitten my lip.

What did the plant that sat in the Maths lesson grow?
Square roots!

Teacher: Hands up anyone who can tell me the name of the first woman on earth. I'll give you a clue: apples.
Alec: Was it Granny Smith, miss?

Why didn't the polar bear eat the penguin?
He couldn't get the wrapper off!

Mother zebra to baby zebra: "No dear, we can't afford a new Arsenal strip. You'll just have to support Newcastle like the rest of us!"

Treble-decker sandwich

Get home from your first day, starving!
Want something to celebrate? Something a bit different?
Try this treble-decker sandwich!

You will need:
Three slices of bread (brown or white to suit!)
Butter or margarine
Fillings: jam, cheese, lettuce, ham, peanut butter, sliced tomatoes, cucumber, crisps, bacon (cooked), mayonnaise, ketchup, tuna, lemon curd, pickle!
Sharp knife

All you need to do:
Choose your two favourite fillings.
Spread butter or margarine on the bread.
Put one filling on the bottom layer.
Cover with a slice of bread.
Put second filling on top.
Place slice of bread on top.
Cut in half.

Eat with care! Enjoy!

The It's Your Move! holiday!

Moving on to any new situation can be quite scary. To meet up with others facing the same challenge can make it seem a lot less difficult. That's why a crowd of nearly 20 young people, who were going to move on to secondary school in six weeks time, went away to Irthlingborough for three days and two nights. They had a brilliant time canoeing and raft-building, abseiling and climbing high ropes, building camp fires and playing weird, wild and wacky games. And they discovered the adventures of Abraham in the Bible who moved onto new things PLUS the bonus of sharing with others who were also preparing for 'moving on up'. Their leaders listened, talked, laughed and gave them some wise advice.

One parent said of the *It's Your Move!* holiday, "Ruth had a great time. Her only complaint was that it was so short."
One girl said, "Brilliant fun! It really helped me get ready for secondary school."

More holidays are planned for this summer. For details, contact www.scriptureunion.org.uk/holidays or holidays@scriptureunion.org.uk

A few weeks to go!

Hannah Hussein

I'll miss the teacher with red hair!

I go to Mellor Primary School in Leicester. I think I will miss Mellor quite a lot, as I have been there almost all my life. I will miss all my teachers and my friends that are not going to my secondary school. I think I will be OK moving to a new school. We have started to move classes for different lessons but nowhere near as many as we'll have to at secondary school.

I am looking forward to meeting new friends. At Mellor, I will miss my teachers and my friends, but most of all the funny things like when my teacher Jon was running and he slipped over. Or when he dyed his hair red. Another thing I will miss is calling the teachers by their first names.

Before I leave Mellor, I am going to make an autograph book in which I will have as many signatures as possible so I will have a memory of everyone.

From the Scottish Islands

Hannah, Iain and Laura live on the Isle of Benbecula, in Western Scotland. They will be going to Sgoil Lionacleit (Liniclate Secondary) which is nearly six kilometres along the coast road from where they live. In the summer term they spent an induction week in the school.

Hannah Beattie has been to four primary schools, so she is used to being a new girl. She looks forward to having different subjects and teachers throughout the day. She isn't looking forward to getting up forty-five minutes earlier to catch the bus!

Iain MacVicar has an older brother at Sgoil Lionacleit. He knows what to expect. He will miss being just five minutes away from home, but looks forward to the wide selection of food in the school cafeteria. Iain thought that knowing

Jesus would be important if he got bullied because Jesus would know what was going on even if other people didn't believe him.

Laura Whittaker has Down's syndrome and she has a learning support assistant with her all the time. She'll need lots of help at first to get used to her new school. She enjoyed the induction week and after the second day, she was able to go to the bus stop on her own. She made a new friend, a boy who has similar difficulties. She is looking forward to meeting him again and getting to know her other classmates.

The coolest bit of the uniform is the tracksuit!

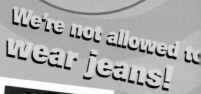

"My name is James Bruce and I have just finished my last year at Pond Park Primary School. I will be heading off to Wallace High School, Lisburn, near Belfast, in September and am looking forward to starting a new school year there.

What I am most looking forward to is meeting new people and doing new things like Food Technology, Biology, Technology and other stuff that I haven't done before. I'm scared of being the smallest in the school again – in case I get bullied – but I hope that won't happen. There will only be one other person from my primary school in my new class, so I guess I'll have to make some new friends.

The uniform makes me feel like I'm going to work in an office. I've got to wear a tie with house colours on it which I don't suppose I'll wear anywhere else really. I am a Christian, so I'll ask God to help me not be scared."

We're not allowed to wear jeans!

Sheryn

"I'm going to Yardley School in Birmingham," says Sheryn Macintosh. "The uniform is a green jumper, black or green trousers or skirt and a white shirt. The shoes we wear are loafers.

I feel excited and very sad because I am going to leave all my friends behind. But my personality is cheerful, outgoing and determined so I'm looking forward to meeting new friends. I will miss all the extra days off and being able to go off to the loo during lesson times. Changing school is a big challenge but I feel I can trust God in everything I do!"

Rebekah Muir

Rebekah Muir (11) goes to Lairdsland Primary, Kirkintilloch near Glasgow. She is really looking forward to starting at Lenzie Academy after the summer. She says, "I moved school two years ago and I was a bit worried then about making friends. But I needn't have worried because I quickly made friends with Rosie and Alexandrea who were put in my work-group!" Rosie and Alexandrea will be moving up with Rebekah, and her big sister is already at the school.

Rebekah enjoys gymnastics, playing the recorder and flute, and loves to draw cartoons. "I am a 'Buddy' to three Primary 1s and that's a bit scary, but I do enjoy being one of the older ones. We have a Scripture Union group in our school every Thursday – it's fun, and sometimes I bring my friends. We hear stories from the Bible and discover just how much God loves us.

"I'm a bit worried about going to Lenzie Academy, which has over 1,300 students. I'll be starting at the bottom again! I'm a bit worried about all the work I'll have to do, but because I know God helped me when I moved before, I know I needn't worry and can trust him to be with me in the future! I'm looking forward to art and technology classes and to seeing what clubs I might join. I know there is an SU group and I'm looking forward to being a part of that."

My sister's there already

"Hi, my name is Joshua Uitterdijk – weird second name, but hey, I live with it! In September, I will be moving to Bishops High School in Chester. Most of my friends are not going there but I chose it because it is very friendly and the teachers seem really nice.

I should know because my sister, Anya, started there last year. My teacher tells us that we will get lots of homework but I know that the amount isn't really frightening. My sister has told me the teachers' nicknames, what the lunch system is, what the timetable is like and what the subjects are. I am worried about bullying, but Anya has told me that they are really strict and work hard not to let it happen.

I don't think I will miss my primary school that much. I have prayed once or twice about getting into the school and my best friend getting in. God answered the prayers, because we're both going to the same school. If things worry me when I am there, I know I can pray about them. And I am looking forward to lots of clubs after school. I want to join the rock-climbing club."

Two years later, this is what Joshua says about the first few days at his new school:

* I did turn up to lessons late because I couldn't find every classroom. But the teachers were very lenient in the first half-term. Generally they are really nice. A few are a bit too strict.
* I didn't get a lot of homework in the first term and I still don't!
* I didn't get round to joining the rock-climbing club but I did join the football club and I have signed up to go skiing in January. There are lots of clubs to join – table tennis, football, netball, hockey, tennis, rock climbing, choir, handbell ringers and keyboard.
* The best thing about being at my school is that you don't just have one teacher throughout the year but one for every subject. The worst thing is that we have a really horrible uniform. I wish I could wear my own clothes to school.
* I don't bump into my sisters a lot.
* I worried about making friends but I needn't have done. I quickly made lots of friends.

My brother's coming!

A year later!

"Hi! My name is Anya. I am twelve years old and I started at Bishops High School, Chester, last September. It is a medium-sized high school and pretty normal, except that it is a Church of England school. Most of the children who go aren't Christians. My friends aren't but they are OK about me being a Christian, although sometimes it's hard.

All the time I was in my junior school, I thought I would go to the high school closest to my home, which is where all my friends were going. But, in Year 6, when we went to look around all the schools, I really liked the friendly atmosphere of Bishops. It was a hard choice to leave my best friends and it has not always been easy for me through the year. But now at the end of Year 7, I am glad about the choice I have made and the new friends I am making.

My teacher in Year 6 was always saying how hard the homework would be and that worried me. But the homework is really not that bad. I was also worried about bullying but Bishops is really strict about that. Sometimes it's hard being the oldest child in the family because I have to go into things first. Everything is unfamiliar and unknown and I can't look to an older brother or sister. It will be easier for my brother, Joshua!

My advice to anyone changing schools is: Don't change into somebody else to make friends. Just be yourself!"

My mum teaches there!

"Hi! My name is Hannah Smith and I am twelve years old and go to Watford School for Girls. When you start at a new school you don't know everyone so you have to make friends. I didn't have any problems making friends but on the first day I didn't know anyone in my form.

My mum teaches RS at the school and is Head of Year 11. Two of my friends have mothers working there too! I think it is fun having a mum as a teacher because she knows what I am doing during exams and also knows my teachers well. If I ever need anything, I can go and see her.

My school offers a lot to the pupils and I enjoy going to Fencing one lunchtime a week. My school is huge and I kept getting lost in the first week, even though I had been there with my mum when I was younger.

My advice to anyone changing schools is: Don't get upset about going to another school as it is fun and you can still keep in touch with your old friends."

What to take on your first day

Rachel Anderson goes to St Joan of Arc Roman Catholic School, in Rickmansworth. This is what she advises you to take on your first day:

"A pencil case containing a pencil, pen, ruler, rubber, sharpener and ink eraser, plus lunch (or money to buy your lunch) and paper, both lined and plain. The teachers will tell you about anything else you'll need."

And she's got some good advice about homework:

"You will get a lot of homework so it's better to get it done the night you get it. Then you get the weekend free to relax."

I didn't get my first choice school!

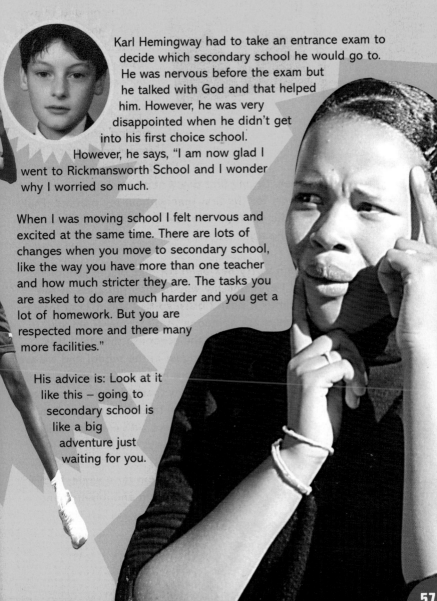

Karl Hemingway had to take an entrance exam to decide which secondary school he would go to. He was nervous before the exam but he talked with God and that helped him. However, he was very disappointed when he didn't get into his first choice school.

However, he says, "I am now glad I went to Rickmansworth School and I wonder why I worried so much.

When I was moving school I felt nervous and excited at the same time. There are lots of changes when you move to secondary school, like the way you have more than one teacher and how much stricter they are. The tasks you are asked to do are much harder and you get a lot of homework. But you are respected more and there many more facilities."

His advice is: Look at it like this – going to secondary school is like a big adventure just waiting for you.

My name is Reuben Johnston and I have just transferred from Strandtown Primary to Sullivan Upper School in Holywood.

I found it quite easy moving from one school to another. But it did involve some changes. On my first day, I had to use public transport for the first time without my parents. That was quite exciting. The bus driver made sure we got off at the right stop.

My main worry has been the size of the school. Would I ever find my way to the right class at the right time? It hasn't been so bad and if I get lost, I can always ask someone to direct me. (I am still finding new parts of the school to this day.) It is strange being the youngest in the school and we are expected to be a bit more mature. (Sometimes that's difficult!) It's good to know that although I am at a big school with lots of new faces, I don't need to worry because Jesus is always with me. I can talk to him wherever I am. He'll always listen.

Now that I have been at Sullivan for a while, I have made new friends and settled in and am enjoying myself.

In the spotlight!

Year 7 tutor
(Guidance teacher)

Name: David Weeks
Age: Middle-aged
School: Chosen Hill Comprehensive School, Churchdown, Gloucestershire
Subject: Geography
Likes: Gliding, ballooning and surfing
Fave food: Strawberries and cream – reminds me of summer days!

Worst classroom experience:
"Telling a pupil to stop banging his desk. 'It's an earthquake, Sir!' he said. And he was right!"

Words of wisdom
Don't believe the horror stories of heads being flushed down loos. They are not true!

Top teacher tips
Make sure you are organised. Then life will be easier for you and everyone else.
Never be afraid to ask for help, and talk to someone you can trust before problems get worse.

Assemblies
I ask God for help when I have to do a scary assembly in front of two hundred pupils. He also gives me the right words to say when I'm talking with someone about bullying or misunderstandings at home. This year in assemblies I talked about street children. Pupils were so concerned, they wanted to know what could be done. We talked about how important it is to know that God cares for everyone, including street children.

Last words
Always make an effort to make new friends. Don't just stick with the old ones.

Form tutor
(Guidance teacher)

Name: Alison Woodward
Age: 30
School: St Paul's Roman Catholic
            School, Milton Keynes
Subject: Italian and French. Currently
            a Year 10 form tutor too.
Fave food: Pasta with anything (well,
            nearly!)
Likes: Hockey, skiing, travelling

My first day at secondary school

I had a nice new uniform (including trendy navy-blue tank top) and a VERY large bag! I expected secondary school to be just like Grange Hill on TV and I remember being disappointed that my school didn't have any stairs.

Words of wisdom

Tutors or teachers do actually want to help you settle in – they don't just shout for the sake of it!

Make the effort to speak to the other people in your form group and in other classes. Don't just hang around with those from your previous school. Also, be aware of other students who may have just moved to the area and do not know anybody – make sure you include them.

What not to do!

Make sure you know what you need for the first day. However, you don't have to buy brand new trainers, every type of pen available, all the latest software packages, a new computer, the whole of W H Smith, etc…

First impressions last a long time, so make sure yours are good for organisation, presentation and behaviour. Your aim should not be to establish yourself as the toughest, roughest, loudest member of the year group!

Top teacher tips

This is your chance to make a fresh start – make a stand for what you know is right. Make the most of new opportunities. Go along to clubs and try out new activities.

Don't forget!

There are many people you can turn to for help or for a chat. Remember that God is one of them. I often pray as I drive to work (with my eyes open, I must add!) to ask for his strength and help.

When you visit your new school there are some key things to do:

- Make notes and write down everything you need to remember.
- Behave in a way that won't get you noticed too quickly.
- Try to get to know one or two other pupils in your new form.
- Find out about:
  the layout of the school
  where the toilets are
  your timetable
  the uniform
  the time you should arrive each morning
  where the drinks and chocolate machines are (let's get our priorities right!!).

If these issues aren't raised, ask questions to make sure you know all you need to know.

The Induction

Homework Timetable

Monday	Tuesday	Wednesday	Thursday	Friday

✆ Scripture Union is an international Christian charity

working in more than 130 countries. Christians believe that their faith in Jesus is important and affects how they live their lives every day. So Scripture Union employs and supports schools workers in local schools to lead assemblies, take RE lessons and act as a listening ear to students of all ages. Scripture Union runs holidays and camps for children and young people and publishes books for young people, including *One Up* (see below). If you'd like to find out what Christians believe, or more about the work of Scripture Union contact the address below or check out the website on www.scriptureunion.org.uk.

[July – September 2004]

oneUP

What's God doing? | Take a break!

Is death the end?

www.scriptureunion.org.uk/oneup

Bible readings to change your life

ONE UP

is a jeans-back-pocket-friendly guide to help you read the Bible. For a free sample of One Up, send a postcard with your name and address on it to: One Up Free Sample, Scripture Union (address below)

Answer from p6: The Bible is the world's best-selling book. Over 500 million Bibles or extracts of the Bible are distributed worldwide every year!

England and Wales: Scripture Union, 207–209 Queensway, Bletchley, Milton Keynes, England, MK2 2EB. Tel: 01908 856000

Northern Ireland: Scripture Union, 157 Albertbridge Road, Belfast, Northern Ireland, BT5 4PS. Tel: 028 9045 4806

Republic of Ireland: Scripture Union, 87 Lower George's Street, Dun Laoghaire Co, Dublin, Irish Republic. Tel: 01 280 2300

Scotland: Scripture Union, 70 Milton St, Glasgow, Scotland, G4 0HR. Tel: 0141 332 1162

Nick's Last Words for
Survival

1 Preparation

Make sure you take all the equipment you need every day (the My Little Pony lunchbox you had at primary school may need updating!). Have a notebook to jot down important info about school. Check your travel arrangements – walking, cycling, car, bus, helicopter - **BE SAFE**.

2 Punctuality

Arrive on time every morning (preferably alert after a good night's sleep). Carry a timetable with you at all times so you know which class you're supposed to be in and when. This will avoid major embarrassment!

3 Perspective

Secondary school isn't really a 'wild jungle' – more like a zoo with lots of interesting animals, so don't hide behind the friends you already know; make some new ones. The zoo keepers are there to help you, not just to contain you – don't be afraid to ask if you need anything. Beware, there are a few dangerous species (but even they are in cages!).

Nick Jeffery spent three years as a Community Worker with the Royal Navy. He has 12 years of experience as a Christian schools worker. He now sets up projects with the local authority to support pupils who are in their first year at secondary school. He is married with three children and is a mad supporter of Portsmouth Football Club!